HOW TO BUY HAPPINESS WITHOUT CASH

100 REASONS OF HAPPINESS- 50 YOURS & 50 MINE

AIMAN SHEIKH

Copyright © Aiman Sheikh
All Rights Reserved.

ISBN 979-888591052-1

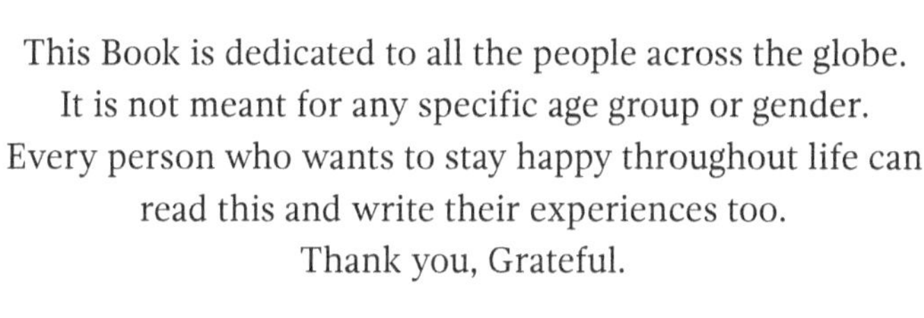

This Book is dedicated to all the people across the globe.
It is not meant for any specific age group or gender.
Every person who wants to stay happy throughout life can
read this and write their experiences too.
Thank you, Grateful.

Contents

Contents

Contents

Part 1

Part 2

Part 3

Part 4

Part 5

Part 6

Part 7

Part 8

Part 9

Part 10

Part 11

Part 12

Part 13

Part 14

Part 15

Preface

How many of us are happy with our lives?

Are you happy right now? Well, I hope you are.

With all these situations happening nowadays, being happy is very expensive, but as the title says, I will help you buy happiness without using your cash. Are you ready?

Well, using your money for happiness is not a loss either.

I have surely not written this book to bore you with any drama or mantras, this book all is yours. You heard it right, it's all yours. I will give you some ideas and you will give some ideas to me.

Let's just help each other to be happy.

Happiness is in your hands. You can make yourself happy. There are more than 100 ways you can be happy. It's not as hard as you may think. These 50 tips will help you start living a happier life today, and the 50 others that you write will make it easy to be happier every day.

Being happy does not mean that everything in your life is perfect or always good but it means you can enjoy the good things that happen to you and be grateful for them. That doesn´t mean you never get sad or upset but it means you don´t let those negative emotions take over your life.

Their are Blank Pages after the end of this Book for you to write about the things that makes you happy.

So, let's get started with our fun journey.

Acknowledgements

I want to thank Miss Priyanka Gupta who once again gave me this opportunity and believed that I can complete this book in a short period and made me complete another Book.

And I want to thank all the people around me who always believed in me and wanted me to write another book with the same energy and enthusiasm.

Always grateful for having good people in my life.

CHAPTER ONE

HAPPINESS

A question that mankind has attempted to answer since the dawn of man. Is a person happy because they have material possessions, or maybe their level of education? These things contribute to one's general happiness but they may not be directly tied to one thing. I believe all people should conduct self-reflection to discover their path to happiness. By discovering what makes you happy, you can more easily adapt your lifestyle to incorporate these activities into your life more often.

Happiness is the one word that defines our lives. But the more you think of happiness, the more confused and puzzled you get. Put your thoughts to rest 'coz here's a book on happiness. You can be happy -every moment of your life. It is your birthright. No one can take it from you. Happiness is a state of mind that is free, able, and available to all.

Ever wondered what everyone's talking about when they say, "I'm so happy!"? Well, this book is here to tell you! Happiness is a feeling of joy and well-being that comes from achievements and accomplishments in one's life. It is a moment of doing something right. It is the glow of living life to the fullest.

In this book, I will mention the chemicals that help to activate happiness hormones.

Do you know what those chemicals are? Do you know what those hormones are? Don't make such a face, I know you are worried about how are chemicals going to help us in being happy. Lol, I wish I can add the laughing emoji here.

The chemicals are:

Dopamine; The reward chemical.

Oxytocin: The love hormone.

Serotonin; The Mood stabilizer.

Endorphin; The Pain Relief Hormone.

It's getting boring right? Let's not waste more time on the introduction and let's get started with our happiness journey.

Reminder: THEIR ARE BLANK PAGES FOR THE READERS AFTER THE END OF THIS BOOK TO WRITE ABOUT THE REASONS THAT MAKES THEM HAPPY.

CHAPTER TWO

SLEEPING

Let's be honest about it. Don't we all love sleeping? Of course, a big Yes. Because happiness is Sleeping peacefully till you wake up with puffy eyes and feel like oh no, I need to sleep more.

Happiness is knowing that it's only 3 AM, I just saw a bad dream and I can sleep more for hours.

Sleep is something we do when we are tired, but did you know that it's important in feeling happy? Your body begins to produce feel-good chemicals like serotonin and dopamine while you are asleep. The next time you want to feel good, put yourself to sleep!

You already knew that happiness can't be bought. But you didn't know that it's free. And the best news is, it comes in a pill form. Nevermind, use only in case of Insomania Or, you can get it for free! It's called sleep. All you need to do is go to sleep and you're happy.

It is hard to be happy without getting enough sleep. There are two kinds of people: the sleepers and the non-sleepers. The non-sleepers are always grumpy and they get little sleep because they lack sleep to be happy.

So why not sleep early if you are sad?

Why sleep till late evenings like a bear?

So, why be sad when you can sleep anytime you want, no doubt there might be a lot of work pressure and all but sleeping is cost-free, just go for it. GO I SAID.

CHAPTER THREE

EATING

I know you smiled. ;)

Who does not love Eating? I mean not the usually dal chawal roti but the pizzas and burgers, the momos and sandwiches, the French fries, the chicken rolls make my eyes get big and my smile gets wide.

Well, a fact here I found on Google is; Scientists can turn peanut butter, into diamonds. (So why not eat and make yourself look like one.)

I repeat, Eat more, be happy. (a little weird I know.) I'll explain it to you. Eat food that makes your body happy. The cyclic ketogenic diet has been shown to increase levels of the neurotransmitter serotonin, which is the chemical that makes you happy. Therefore theoretically if you eat a cyclic ketogenic diet you should be happy! But don't take my word for it, research "how does eating more help in being happy."

Eating helps with being happy! Scientists have proven that people who eat smaller amounts throughout the day are happier. When you eat more often, your body makes polypeptide, which is like a hormone that works as an anti-anxiety.

Well, i honestly have no idea who these scientists are but whatever they have said is not wrong either?

So, why be sad when you can eat anything you want, the chocolates, the ice creams, the veg rolls, the Biryani, and whatnot.

CHAPTER FOUR

COOKING

It's obvious when you want to eat you've to cook sometimes too because nothing tastes better than homemade. Cooking is the art, science, and discipline of preparing and presenting food. Also when the food comes out tasty nothing can make us happy than the compliments we receive for the tasty food we cook.

We all know that food tastes better when it's cooked on the grill. The smell gets your mouth watering before you bite into a juicy burger or vegetable kebob. But did you know that eating grilled food can make you happy?

If you love to cook and if you love food and you love eating, then why wouldn't you be happy? Cooking is a passion for me, the smell and the taste of good food is the best in the world. It gives me happiness that I can not describe, a warm fuzzy feeling in my tummy. I do not know a more desirable thing in this world than to cook something delicious at home just because I want to show it off to all my friends and family I am so happy when my dear ones tell me how delicious it was.

I will keep this chapter precise because i know most of us are too lazy to cook and read too.

So, why be sad when you can cook, get up and cook some fresh food and make your tummy and yourself happy.

CHAPTER FIVE

SINGING

Any song in your head right now? Let's admit it, we all are secret bathroom singers, right? And at least once in our lives, we felt like "Woah", I am not that bad at singing and the recording after that ruined the dream, haha.

Remember the school picnics, when we used to sing throughout the journey and the best part of the picnic was the singing part only?

Some people think that singing can help you in being happy. Sometimes when you sing, you might forget about the problems that you had. As a result, you would feel good. If you sing alone or with friends, you would feel great about it too. When things get cheerful, why don't you sing too? This book will let you know and show more about the importance of singing and how it could positively affect your personality.

Singing helps in being happy because it makes you forget everything else. You ignore all things and just follow your passion. While singing, you don't stop to think of any problem or negativity. You just enter the world of music and party all the way. Singing has a lot of health benefits too that make you feel relaxed.

I am writing down the facts I have been reading since the day I thought of writing this book. Please be patient.

So, why be sad when you can sing anything, anytime, in any situation in your head only?

CHAPTER SIX

DANCING

Well, I am sure you all know how dancing helps in being happy. But there must not be too many people who actually do know about it. So I thought to share my thoughts on this topic.

You know when we're alone and some dance songs are playing and we forget about everything else and start moving our body with music. That moment when we don't even know what we're doing but the relief of nobody is watching is on the top of the world and we don't stop and keep moving until we feel like stop this is not what I am supposed to do, I was supposed to worry about why I was sad and anxious but then you feel like no I should do more. The most important thing is that Dancing also reduces stress and tension for the mind and body.

Dancing makes you happy. It helps your life in many ways. When you dance, you feel more energetic and active. In addition to that, it integrates you mind together with your body. Also, you enjoy doing that with others. This activity gives you a sense of connectedness to other people. As a result, you are highly motivated to do various activities in life with the people around you, including work at school and play time with friends.

While being happy is a subjective term, dancing has been proven to many people it helps bring out their happiness! Dancing relieves stress and improves mood, therefore leading to an increase in happiness. It also boosts stamina and makes you feel more passionate about life. The list goes on and on, but please just give dancing a try...you'll be happy you did!

So, why be sad when you can dance and increase your muscle strength and improve your moves too.

CHAPTER SEVEN

EXERCISE

Do you sometimes feel like your heart isn't working properly and Does it feel like there is something heavy there? No, it's not because of any heartbreak. It's only because of the lack of exercise. Exercises can boost your mood within no time, you feel energetic and powerful. Exercise strengthens your heart and improves your circulation. So, next time when feeling low exercise a bit and memorize what I said, it's not heartbreak, you lack exercise.

Exercise can do so much for your self-worth and happiness. I changed my views on my body, because of all the exercise I was doing. In other words, my body was no longer disgusting. I went from having no self-confidence, to loving myself. Exercise can make you a happier person, by having more positive thoughts about yourself.

Exercise helps in being happy. It makes you feel better about your body....yup it's that simple.

So, why be sad, when you can exercise and kick all the sadness away?

CHAPTER EIGHT

COMPLIMENT

Since compliments are FREE, why aren't we using them? Just get up, Yes I am talking to you only, get up and look at the mirror and see how beautifully you're crafted by the Lord. How pretty are your eyes, how they shine when they look up into the sky? When you see someone walking around, go to them and say, "HEY, YOU'RE THE MOST PRETTIEST PERSON I HAVE EVER SEEN, GOD BLESS YOU" and look at their eyes how big and bright they will look. And boom, you made someone's day. You're already a Star. And Guess What its free of cost,

Because when you're happy and you know it, compliment someone. Show your appreciation and make the world a happier place. Compliments should be well thought out and delivered spiritedly. Complimenting someone makes you happy. It is a type of Praise, and praise makes people feel good about themselves. Knowing that someone thinks you did a good job can make you feel proud. People like to feel good about themselves. Knowing that someone thinks you are smart or attractive doesn't mean you have to agree with them.

So, why be sad? When you can complemint and make anyone's day.

CHAPTER NINE

SMILE

A smile is the universal sign of happiness. Why are you smiling? Hey, don't stop just smile you look beautiful. Smile every time, everywhere you go. Because it's easier to smile than to frown. Also, Smiling can reduce your Blood pressure. What are you waiting for then?

Everyone knows that a smile is contagious. A smile makes those around you feel good. So why not smile? Smiling is much better for you than yelling in anger or expressing frustration through silence. So if you have a choice, choose to smile!

Why go for medicines when you can just smile and make it all look happier. No matter how your teeth look crooked, non-aligned, or straight just smile, it is the best natural makeup you all need. Smiling is important! It makes you happy, but mostly it makes everyone else around you happier. It's sort of like an instant mood-booster.

Well, who doesn't love the feeling of having a nice smile on one face? The best part is that it's not difficult at all to let a smile appear on your face. The more you smile the more happy you become, just accept it everyone smiles when they become an adult.All you need to do is keep yourself happy and start smiling at others!

So, why be sad when you can Smile as wide as you can.

CHAPTER TEN

SELF CARE

What's self-care for you?

Wait let me guess, self-care for you is skincare right? The manicure, pedicures, face masks, packs, and scrubs?

Well, a big no.

Self-care has 8 main areas: Physical, psychological, emotional, social, professional, environmental, spiritual, and financial. When all these things are stable there will be no reason to be sad, not a single one.

Self-care can maintain self-confidence and self-esteem. It makes us more aware of our personal needs.

When you take care of yourself, that's when happiness begins. And who doesn't want to be happy? So I will tell you how it helps and what the benefits are. You there! Hey, you over there! Don't pretend to pay attention to me, I can see that you're looking out at me, so I know that you can hear me too.

Anyway, self-care is one of the secrets to happiness and it also helps to lighten depression because when you took care of yourself and feel good about yourself as well as digest things calmly when something bad happens and hence getting rid of stress, don't you agree that that's one of the keys to happiness? Let's not drag it because I know you have understood what you have to.

So, why be sad when you can do Self-care and vanish all the sadness away.

CHAPTER ELEVEN

MAKE UP

Did you know, women used to pinch their cheeks to give themselves rosy cheeks before the invention of blush. And we right now have the most beautiful items and some of us don't even use them. Why? Only because we think people might start judging us for wearing too much, too little, too dark, too light make-up? What if they're jealous? What if they don't want to see you look this pretty when you wear their red lipstick and mascara and walk around them. You bought all the items for what? Just to keep them on the cupboard, No honey get up and take the brush and show the world how beautiful you're, with or without makeup.

Let's face it, most women don't use makeup every day. That being said, no one wakes up unhappy-looking perfectly beautiful. Makeup is an art form that has been around for ages, and it is an everyday help to some extent. It doesn't hide your uglies, but it creates a better you, who you can be happy with.

So, why be sad when you can do makeup and roll your eyes with black eyeliner and mascara.

CHAPTER TWELVE

DRESS UP

What did you pretend to be when you were a child? A doctor? An astronaut? A parent? Perhaps you pretended to be a paleontologist, wearing a camouflage vest and digging up "dinosaur bones"? or your mama's old dupatta to look like her and called yourself a bride? No doubt it was the Happiest era of your life. But where did that go? Why did you stop doing that, why don't you dress like how you always wanted to do? Life is too short to think I shouldn't wear this or that because this or that particular person won't like it, so get up and dress up however you want.

Don't worry about the people who say, why are so you so dressed up! Just because they don't like it doesn't mean you're not looking cute.

Dressing up could help be happy. Just like the name of the famous game- Angry birds, a person would need to dress up to be angry. You would look much angrier without clothes than you would if you put on your clothes. The same rule even applies to love. Do you want to be loved by someone? You would need to dress up for that. Lol, I have gone too far. Apologies.

So, why be sad when you can Dress up because life is too short to blend in. Don't settle for average.

CHAPTER THIRTEEN

WRITE

Hey, hope you don't mind if I give you some advice. Would you like to be happy? Of course, you would. Well, let me ask you this. How much writing do you do every day? For most people, it's not enough. Most people are not happy because they write too little rather than too much. try writing three pages a day (500 words) and see if you don't notice the difference in your mood. It works for me, and I know it will work for you.

When was the last time you wrote your heart out when you were feeling low and didn't find anything to do but sat down and penned everything that was disturbing you? Might be a long time right?

Writing is something that makes people happy for various reasons. Most people think about writing when experiencing a hard time or even feeling down. So, you need to give writing the chance to show how helpful it can be in your life.

Why not start it again? Let's give it a try at least maybe you'll feel the happiest again when you see yourself getting better at writing your thoughts. Maybe then you can write about people's miseries and happy life also. Maybe you can go a long way with your writing talent. What else do you need to be happy in your life?

So, why be sad when you can write whatever you want because there is no such thing as a bad writer.

CHAPTER FOURTEEN

LEARN

When you hear the word 'learn' you may think of When you take in new information and increase your overall knowledge. This could be through either your own experiences, periods of hard work and study, or by being taught. Although this is true when you learn up complex process it's also behavior place within your body, and you suddenly become happy.

The next time someone asks you how to be happy, tell them that learning new things helps too! Before you know it, they'll be back asking if there's anything else you do to be happy.

Learning can be anything, you can learn new languages, new and old music, dance, makeup, typing, writing, gardening, cycling, driving, and whatnot.

Did you know that your brain is the funniest organ in your body? So it makes sense that we want to keep it happy, right? If you want to be happy, you need to keep doing new things and learning. If you never do anything new, your brain will stop growing and that would just not be cool, man. So let's get started!

I tried keeping this chapter precise too because honestly this is not my favorite thing to do too. I AM BEING

BRUTALLY HONEST.

So, why be sad when you can learn new things all day around.

24

CHAPTER FIFTEEN

READ

I just had thought this chapter should be the first chapter of this book,right?

Anyways, lets not get distracted in the middle.

You know what makes me really happy? Reading. Yes, I know, it's not the coolest thing out there but it is the best thing.

Also, you know what reading protects from prison.

Habitual reading can make you kinder and happier. Reading is a process of talking in the sense or meaning of a letter, especially by sight or touch. Well including more facts here; Reading reduces stress, and no stress means more happiness. Reading can take you to a whole new world.

Don't know what to read, from where to start?

Well, I am still here to guide you.

I will suggest to you the most interesting books you can get your reading start with.

1. The Dairy of a young girl.
2. Harry Potter series.
3. The Alchemist.
4. IKIGAI.
5. PRIDE AND PREJUDICE.

6. How to win friends and influence people.

7. Little women.

8. Animal farm.

9. The kite runner.

10. A tale of two cities.

11. IS IT REALLY LOVE. (You might have never heard about this book, it's the first-ever book I published.) Did I just prompted my first book in my second book lol. Please go and read that one too. Although that book is full of imperfections but it still has got my heart not whole just one chamber.

CHAPTER SIXTEEN

CUT OFF WITH TOXIC PEOPLE

What is a Toxic Person?

A Toxic Person is someone with whom you feel you're being manipulated into something you don't want to. Also, you're constantly confused by the person's behavior. And you never feel fully comfortable around this person.

Most of us keep finding the reason to cut off some people who are toxic but it doesn't feel easy, because they come back every time you try to remove them from your life and nothing makes a person sadder, now let's make it easier.

Consider distance rather than complete removal.

Yes, some negative relationships, such as friends and colleagues can be improved simply by creating space. When you see or talk to them less often, you'll remove yourself from their dynamic stop fanning the flames.

Some of the tips I learned from the internet because happiness matters and Toxic people don't.

1. Avoid playing into their reality.

2. Don't get drawn in.

3. Pay attention to how they make you feel.

4. Talk to them about their behavior.

5. Put yourself first.

6. Offer compassion, but don't try to fix them.

7. Say no and walk away.

8. Remember, you aren't at fault.

So, why be sad when you can remove all the toxic people and be the happiest even if you have to be alone.

CHAPTER SEVENTEEN

MAKE NEW FRIENDS

NOT HAVING ANY FRIENDS CAN BE DANGEROUS TO YOUR HEALTH. (Just a happy reminder).

Friends bring more happiness into our lives than virtually anything else. Friendships also have a huge impact on your mental health and happiness

If you ever start feeling you're losing friends or people don't want to stay connected with you, just be okay with it. Maybe they don't get along with you, maybe don't have the similar taste as you do, or maybe they're not meant to be in your life as friends. You can make friends anywhere, bet it your new school, the coffee shop, the bus stand, Facebook, Instagram, or wherever you're available. Just smile and show them your happy face and there you're friends now.

Try interacting with new people, meet new people. The first stage of friendship is Contact.

Contact involves meeting someone and forming early impressions of him or her.

Now, the question here is why new friends?

1. New friends can help you to open yourself to new possibilities.

2. New friends help you teach new things.

3. New friends are a source of New entertainment.

4. Last, not least it's a fresh start.

So, why be sad when you can make new friends all over the globe.

CHAPTER EIGHTEEN

Does planning make you happy?

You plan a vacation, you plan a walk, you plan your birthday, you plan a party... You are so into planning things that it can't be looked at as a bad habit.

I feel like when you plan a trip with your friends and then for the whole night you stay awake just to go and enjoy, the butterflies you feel in your stomach all the time when you plan to buy a new dress when you plan to save for the whole month to buy that pair of shoes?

Every day, people plan for things. They plan for their birthday parties and maybe even their wedding. They plan to get married, but they don't plan to get divorced. Ooops, sorry. Planning is cool because it helps you really think about what's coming up in the future. It'll help you be happier because planning makes you think about what to do now so that later you won't get sad 'cause something happened.

Isn't this happiness?

Plan things like;

1. Scan the Day for the positive.
2. Form your intention to be happy.
3. Make a happy commitment.
4. Nourish.
5. Plan one thing towards your goal.
6. Plan for a good sleep.

So, why be sad when you can Plan for happiness.

CHAPTER NINETEEN

DITCH YOUR PHONE

(for some time obviously)

Phone; it's something most of us can't live without, obviously we can but we feel like it.

And it is the most important factor that leads us to sadness without even realizing how badly it influences us sometimes. It can take away your happiness because the internet has all the fake things, and people in it. That can lead you to feel low and self-doubt thing.

Now you might be thinking we have always tried to do this but couldn't make it happen because we always end up taking our phone, opening chats, scrolling miles with our thumb, and wasting time. Why not giving it a real try this time...

Do you know, Mobiles phones are dirtier than toilet handles? I don't know the fact behind it but I think it can be one reason to avoid it though! Haha.

Want to know some facts? Let's see some;

1. Pause to think before picking up your phone.

2. Analyze how you use your phone and set limits.

3. Get rid of distracting apps.

4. Minimize notifications.

5. Keep your phone away.

6. Stop using your phone before going to bed.

So, why be sad when you can ditch your phone and have fun in your life.

CHAPTER TWENTY

TRAVELLING

Travelling has many benefits and helps in getting rid of stress and achieving happiness. I learned that traveling is fun and relaxing. It keeps me refreshed and happy. It helps me explore new places, meet new people and learn many things that I wouldn't have learned if I was at home. While traveling, I stopped caring about my house, my car, or even the clothes I wore! It is a way to enjoy life by making the most of its simple pleasures.

How many of us want to travel but study pressure, home chores don't let us fulfill the dream. Yes, money is also a problem, Lol. But traveling doesn't only mean, Dubai, Europe, the USA and all. You can travel to some local garden, to the lake near your home or go for tracking in the mountains. How beautiful and powerful does it sound? Isn't it enough to make your soul happy?

If not this what else can make us happy then.

CHAPTER TWENTY-ONE

ART

Many of us love doing Art. Many of us are so great at it. We make Paintings of Humans, nature, animals, and whatever comes to our minds. Art refreshes everything around us. Yes, it may be a little messy but the result is always worth the mess.

Now the question here is why should we start doing art and painting to be happy? Well, maybe when you paint a picture, you feel contentment and calm. No matter what the scene is, the colors can bring you to your childhood's land. It's like a drug. When you paint, you're on a journey into your mind.

This is because the process of learning art and painting can be very fun, which will make you excited. That is to say, there is a lot of things that we can learn from our failures in painting. The more we fail, the more we are learning. And then we find the happiness of doing art and creating our artworks.

If there is something that we should start doing, it's painting. And I'm not saying this because I'm an artist, or because I think my art skills are unbelievable. It's just that unlike other hobbies like tennis or soccer, arts and painting never get tedious. You always have new things you can learn, and even the masters before us had to go through a long process to become great artists.

So, you know what I am about to say!!! Do you want to repeat it with me?

Why be sad when you can do art and make yourself a little happy world.

CHAPTER TWENTY-TWO

DRIVE

Wait, you have a license, right?

No, wait you are above 18, right?

No, no stop you know how to drive right?

Please don't blame me, if you get caught.

Alright, we all love car rides right? Not necessarily the car, it can be a bicycle, a scooter, or anything that we can ride on. Sometimes all you need is a space where you can be alone with yourself just to make yourself feel happy and remove the anxiety from your mind, it can be the best thing to do so.

Finding happiness by driving can seem bizarre, but it's true. A lot of people do indeed find being out on the road makes them very happy.

Drive for your happiness. When you drive with the Honda, the moment of arriving is a joyous occasion and a whole new experience! It feels like the first time every time. Drive for your happiness!

Most people think that if they obtain a luxury car that costs a 5million or more, they can get happiness. The fact is wrong although we have a car which costs 5million on the one hand and we have 0 money on other hand. So why be broken we can enjoy a 20k scooter's ride and be happy with our lives without being broken. Yes, I know you might be thinking we don't even have that 20k in our pockets, have you ever heard of a thing called rent? Lol, yes? go for it and enjoy.

So, are you ready?

Why be sad when you drive the world crazy, oops inappropriate word, but who cares?

CHAPTER TWENTY-THREE

WALK

I just love to go for long walks, it helps me to enjoy things that I never noticed before. Do you?

We should know that going for a walk gives us more happiness and joy. Here is why: We should know that walking is good for our health, it is good for our body and mind. It's just like sleeping immediately after studying a lot before an exam.

Walking helps to keep us fit during the summer. Stepping out of your house on a beautiful day will give you some fresh air and sunlight which are necessary for your body. The sun helps in releasing vitamin D which is good for healthy skin, bones, and even the heart. You will feel relaxed after you have walked a long way especially if you have not gone outside your house ever since you came home from school/office or sometimes even home town.

Uninterrupted walking will also help clear your stress as well as help your body relax too, once you are finished with the walk. Umm, I am sure it's not getting boring right? I just wanted to ask never mind. Can't add an emoji.

You walk out of your house and you are happy, you have a dog as a pet and you are happy, you take food and you eat then you are happy. So walk for some time get happiness.

So, you ready?

Why be sad when you can get up and walk in nature and make yourself feel happy.

41

CHAPTER TWENTY-FOUR

CALL SOMEONE YOU LOVE

How often do we feel lonely even if we know that there are so many people out there, the ones we call our friends, family, relatives, or anyone we connect with. But whenever we are sad or we do not feel happy we just want someone to be there with whom we can share our feelings. The feelings that even we don't know why we feel? I am writing it, right? Of course, I am.

Sometimes we just want someone to be there and feel our silence and keep us calm. This is the best feeling in the world, don't doubt it. Yes, it is.

The real reason why we call people we love to feel happy is that it can control the size of our pupils and make us in a better mood.

We should call people we love because they make us feel happy in many ways. When you go through hard times it is nice to talk to someone, who will listen. So if you are having troubles and not feeling good call someone you love, a parent an older sibling, or even a best friend.

We should love and cherish our family and friends because they are there for us when we need them, they love us and care that we are safe. That is why they are called "Family" when they care so much about you and worry if you are doing well and keeping safe.

So, why be sad when you can call your loved one anytime anywhere? They really Love you right? I am not supposed to say this here. Bye.

CHAPTER TWENTY-FIVE

TALK TO YOUR BEST FRIEND

If you truly think talking to your best friend will make you sad, then please phone the Samaritans, or you need to change your best friend. I really mean it. Talking to your best friend has enormous positive effects on the brain. It can improve your mood and ability to learn, significantly decrease anxiety and depression, improve your social and problem-solving skills, and much more.

We are always trying to know everything about happiness. Your best friend can help. Have you ever stopped and spoken to your best friend to ask if he or she was happy? Chances are you probably don't—but why?

Everyone knows that sharing secrets is what best friends are for. But it turns out, we have another best friend who's even better at making us feel good: our pets. Research shows that a dog's and cat, cuddly presence can trigger your brain to release oxytocin, a hormone that promotes bonding and well-being. And with no awkward texting or dating, it's easy to get some warm fuzzies with your best four-legged buddy.

I have so much to write about this chapter but let me stop here because I don't want it to get boring.

So, why be bored when you have a best friend, get boring with them, play, and share your whole heart with them.

CHAPTER TWENTY-SIX

TAKE PICTURES

I know right? You are not photogenic, I understand the pain because neither am I friends. Sigh!

But who cares? We don't Take Pictures to show people, we don't right? I mean maybe we do but we are beautiful like we the way we are, I am not a good motivational coach but I try, sometimes. But during the process of taking pictures, we try everything to be happy, but the pictures would not tell this. The pictures are just frozen memories. It is only when you look back and see them, it means they are something that can make you happy. Why keep taking pictures? Because it is your way of explaining what you want others to understand.

Taking pictures literally adds meaning to the phrase, "a picture is worth a thousand words." Research has found that when people take pictures of activities they enjoy doing, their overall well-being increases. Therefore, the next time you plan an event, keep snapping pictures throughout the event and after as this will significantly improve your overall mood. I don't know who all keep doing these researches though. Lol.

So, why be sad when you can get up, get ready and Take countless pictures.

CHAPTER TWENTY-SEVEN

SAVE MONEY

Do you know the feeling when you find an old note in an old diary?

That million-dollar smile. Well, not now because if today we find any old note in our old diaries or books we won't be happy but we will cry. All the Indians can relate, can't add an emoji but blah.

If you save money, you'll be happy. If you're happy, you'll love your life. If you love your life, then what else is there? To be sure that we are all on the same page, let's go through it point by point:

Happiness while saving money is something out of the world. Even if it is only a hundred bucks the happiness is worth a million and the proud moment too.

Why don't we do a thing, whenever we feel sad and save a buck in a piggy bank or anywhere you feel it will be safe because there is a species called siblings in the home too.

We have been taught that everything we need to be happy can be purchased. We live in a time of enormous debt in this world, and given the opportunity to write a column about ways to save money, I ask you: Why should we save money? You can write it down on the next page.

So, whenever you feel sad save a buck for your happiness. Someone has told me that they hate when people call it bucks not paisa. But Paisa does not make us happy it's Bucks and Bucks and Million of Bucks.

CHAPTER TWENTY-EIGHT

SPEND MONEY

Now that you have saved the money, why not spend it for making ourselves happy? You spend money to buy things that make you happy, so you can be happier.

Proven scientific research suggests that consumption is the secret to happiness, but new research shows that spending money on others rather than on yourself is what makes you happy! So spend it now! In a variety of convenient denominations for the whole family to spend. Only if you have.

Consumption is the secret to happiness, but new research shows that spending money on others rather than on yourself is what makes you happy! So spend it now! In a variety of convenient denominations for the whole family to spend.

Happiness has a price. The big question is: should we spend our hard-earned money on things that will make us happy? I think we should. Purchasing things like experiences, like travel, makes people happier than spending on material goods such as buying an expensive car or new living room furniture. People who buy material things tend to be happier, but there's a catch--You have to enjoy spending time with your family and friends for buying a house to make you happy.

Here is a question for people that say money doesn't buy real happiness. So why do we keep spending more and more?

What are you waiting for then, get up buy yourself that dress and the cake you wanted to eat for so long and be happy with your life.

CHAPTER TWENTY-NINE

HAIR CUT

This is one of the favorite Chapters of mine of this Book.

Because that is what i do, and now i look like a tom boy. I should stop here, i am not here to demotivate you.

Maybe you should cut your hair and keep your happiness.

It sometimes feels so heavy right? Just cut the heaviness off and flaunt your beautiful hair.

For some reason, most of us think that long hair is not only fashionable but also good for every occasion in life. However, when looking at the statistics that are provided by Haircutting Weekly, we can see that long hair does not make happiness. It does exist several facts showing the positive effects of cutting one's hair. You might be curious about what they are, or you might be an expert with long hair who would like to have more information on this topic. Either way, please go on reading!

I am not saying you to cut your whole length or make yourself look like an egg. Don't blame me, please. I am just saying that if it is not feeling good just let it go. Give it a new style, a new cut, a new life.

Let's say it together why be sad when we can cut our hair but wait, go to a salon, please.

CHAPTER THIRTY

WATCH TV

What's your favorite cartoon? Doraemon, Shinchan, or Tom and Jerry only millennials and Gen Z people know. I feel bad for the next generation already. They will never know how happiness was just a TV show, not YouTube Netflix, and chill.

And your favorite movie? It is not Taare Zameen par for sure, I was about to drop an emoji here. Lol.

There are all these amazing movies and cartoons out there! They're developed to make us happy, but we choose not to watch them. Why though? I mean, we've got the time and the internet makes everything so easy to find and watch. Let's delve into how making a habit of watching at least one movie or cartoon a day can bring in some serious happiness and joy.

Let's face it. The only reason that people watch movies or cartoons is that they're happy already! People use these in their leisure time and it creates a positive effect on their moods. To be honest, watching things like this makes people happier than going to the beach because the beach isn't full of funny-looking characters like shin chan and Nobita.

What are you waiting for then? why are you still sad, just switch on the TV and start watching your favorite Show and make your mood happy.

CHAPTER THIRTY-ONE

MAKE YOUR SELF FEEL SPECIAL

When was the last time you treated yourself well, or you said I LOVE YOU to yourself in the mirror? Don't remember hah? That's alright, now is the right time to do it. Because if you can't treat yourself well how can you treat anybody on this earth? If it's you who can't accept yourself, your flaws, you cannot accept the other person happy. I repeat you cannot.

As I sit here sipping my morning coffee, I have been thinking the same thing: Why should I make myself feel special to be happy? Am I not special enough without having to make myself feel so good? Who knows maybe you are asking yourself the same question.

You should make yourself feel special because you are special. It turns out we are all individuals, so therefore we should all feel special.

We all want to feel special, so it feels good when we are treated as if we are. It's part of what makes us human.

Millions of people go to bed every night without finding true happiness. Stories of happiness you can read in newspapers or magazines seem unrealistic. Remember, these are not stories about your life. Your life is about the daily realities in which you live, love and lose, succeed and fail, feel happy and sad, get angry and forgive, get old, and have new memories.

Try to make yourself happy first and then think about the rest of the world. This is not selfishness my friend, but self-love. Start loving yourself first.

Now that we have come so far, you know what to say right?

Why be sad when you can love yourself and make yourself feel happy every second of the day.

CHAPTER THIRTY-TWO

STOP CARING ABOUT WHAT PEOPLE SAY

We all have cried at least once in our life because of what other people think or talk about us. I have almost a thousand times. Lol.

I know this is the worst feeling and it directly affects our mood, happiness, and our health too.

We are conditioned to think that the things that would make us happy are the things that material possessions can buy, but do we have to stop caring about people to be happy? This is a very important question.

What if someone told you not to care about people anymore? Not to care about their feelings, not to care about others' pain. Every day a hundred people you know would die, one by one. A hundred each day for a month. Would you stop caring? Obviously no because you know it's not how your heart is. But what if the same person or the other person says that you can have an alternative to this by not caring about what people say or think about you, what would you say? This is who you are a soft-hearted kind person.

We all care too much, don't we? About what others think and say about us, about what makes them happy and sad instead of our happiness. But why should we stop caring? We should care because we are human beings and being human is a great thing that grants us amazing qualities. But only to the positive energy and things.

So, why are you still sad when you can stop thinking about others' negative things and start living your happy life, because; KUCH TOU LOUG KAHEGE, LOGU KA KAAM HAI KEHNA.

CHAPTER THIRTY-THREE

APOLOGIZE

Do you ever think about the people you have hurt? Do you ever think that the reason you are sad is that somehow, sometimes you may have hurt someone so bad that they can't forget about it? If not then please, think about it at least once and ask your heart, is this right to hurt someone?

Now, if in case you may have hurt someone just apologize. It won't make you feel low nor will it make the other person feel superior. It will just make your heart feel happy and the other person too. You might have that heavy feeling inside you but after you apologize to the person you will feel free. Please do this, please.

On the other hand, It is amazing to think that we sometimes apologize for what makes us happy? We sometimes feel that we have to apologize for being in a really good mood. The words "I'm sorry" escape our lips as we witness a truly awful event on the news or read an upsetting email. We apologize for disagreeing with someone and we feel guilty if we are having a great time at the expense of others.

Let me help you by showing a little Apology sentence;

I apologize for all the terrible things I've said about you in my head. You're making me happy now and I deserve some happiness. If it makes you feel any better I didn't say them out loud – well, a lot of them at least. Phew. I'm so glad that's off my chest! I am sorry please forgive me. Wow, that's it. That's how simple it is. I promise.

So, don't wait to pick up your phone and give a call, or text the person you've hurt and start living a regret-free and happy life.

CHAPTER THIRTY-FOUR

PLAY IN THE RAIN

I know it's not raining outside, but someday, somewhere it will. Promise. Haha, I should not be kidding right now but I can't stop myself. Okay, tell me do you love walking in the rain because no one can see you crying. No stop this is not what I am supposed to do here. Let's start again, do you love watching the rain from your window?

The next time it starts raining wear your long boots and go outside to play in the rain. Trust me you will not regret it. Just trust me. I know you don't but you can.

Have you noticed that kids would much rather play in the rain than stay inside when it's sunny? No, it's not just about learning about the water cycle and how clouds are formed. It's about feeling happy. There's something about getting wet that helps our souls relax and feel lighter, probably because we're so used to being dry most of the time. I hope it is making sense to you all?

Okay, this time you will have to wait.

So, why be sad when you can go out and play in the rain and make yourself wet and happy. Don't catch a cold though.

CHAPTER THIRTY-FIVE

BUY A PET

Uhhh, so here is my favorite chapter, yes my most favorite one.

I am a cat and dog person, although I am always afraid of both in the start the way I get attached to them is unbelievable.

Pets are the most lovable creatures after your friends. Friends are not creatures? No, they are. Okay.

The best way you can treat yourself is to buy a pet for yourself and make the rest of your life happy.

Some people have got the secret to staying happy. They own a pet, who is always there with them and never gets upset with them. Some people think that you should buy a pet because a dog or cat makes a home feel less lonely. If you are thinking about it, then yes, it is true that you should get a dog or cat for your house as pets make homes more colorful. Disney has made an advertisement on how dogs or cats can change our moods by using their brand character "Mickey Mouse". What do you think?

We cannot live with pets and not feel happy. They are a kind of necessity in life because, in presence of pets, people do not feel alone. Pets can also help humans to stay healthy. Pets help heal our souls. We should buy a pet not only because they are cute but they make our life better.

Hey, yes you get up and get yourself a pet, please!!!!

You won't be sad, I promise. You will never be sad with them.

CHAPTER THIRTY-SIX

PLAY WITH KIDS

Most of you will be like, ughh who loves kids? They are annoying. Yes, I know that feeling when they start screaming for no reason and when they don't let you sleep peacefully. But the time when a kid grabs your finger and starts laughing at you and then fell asleep in your lap, what about that. When you feel superior above all and start bragging about that little thing to everyone. Kids can make you feel the happiest.

Playing with kids makes you happy! This fact has been discovered by a British psychologist who tracked the happiness levels of 2,000 people. Huh, you still don't believe me?

Kids make us happy. Anyone who says otherwise is lying because children are tiny bundles of joy and cuteness. They like to giggle, they like to run around, they like to do weird things like point at inanimate objects and make kissy noises at them.

Sometimes we feel so much more productive when we work with kids. But we also play with them to feel happy.

So, no no I am not saying to get a kid, damn. I am just saying play with them, the ones in your neighborhood or your nephew or niece and start seeing a change in your behavior.

CHAPTER THIRTY-SEVEN

CUDDLE WITH YOUR FAVOURITE PERSON

Why are you blushing? I know it's your favorite thing to do when you're sad. Cuddling can increase happiness all around the globe. The best thing about this is you don't have to pay money for it.

Cuddling promotes happiness. Cuddling makes people happy. Cuddling is a source of happiness and joy that you can feel every day, anytime and anywhere. Why should we do cuddling to feel happy? Because it is good for the body, the mind, and the psyche.

Cuddling is an underrated emotional experience that brings great benefits to the happiness and well-being of humans! Cuddling makes your brain happier. It activates the pleasure centers of your brain, lowers levels of the stress hormone cortisol, boosts levels of oxytocin (the "love hormone"), and increases a feeling of connection with other people. Scientists at the University of Zurich and Princeton University found that across cultures, physical touch is our most highly evolved language for expressing and exchanging emotions.

Rest you know right? I hope I am not boring you by saying this thing again and again. (Crying emojis) why be sad when you can cuddle your favorite person and be the happiest of all.

CHAPTER THIRTY-EIGHT

HOLD HANDS

Do you know why we hold hands to feel happy? It's not just a random practice...or is it?

Please read the whole thing first. Holding hands here means that whenever you are feeling low hold hands of the people you trust, the people you love, the people you think care about you. No your duffer or anyone who is walking around.

When the sun rises, we go outside and hold hands with our friends. Why? Because science says so. According to a small Japanese school study, holding hands helps us feel more socially connected. This in turn makes us happier. Scientists say we should hold hands more often! It took me a lot to research, I promise.

By holding hands with a friend or loved one, you can directly transfer a physical sensation of happiness from one person to another.

Don't wait for me just say it on your own.

Why be sad when you can hold your loved one's hands.

It rhymed, yayyy.

CHAPTER THIRTY-NINE

GOSSIP

Are you from your mother's side of the family or your father's side? If I talk about myself whenever I am gossiping with my mother I am from her side, and when I am gossiping with my father I am from his side. This way keeps everything in balance. I know you all relate to this thing.

I think my secret is out now, Damn.

Anytime you feel sad about anything just go to your mother and start gossiping about anything to her and see the dark mode turning to happy mode.

Why gossip? Isn't it a bad thing? At first, we think gossip is just useless talk. But wait a minute! We all gather information through conversations when we chat, quarrel or communicate with others. Through conversations, we will get to know people's attitudes, emotions, feelings, and even their thoughts. Gossip can be useful when used properly.

It is necessary to have a certain amount of information about other people to make friends with them, get along with them, negotiate with them and even work together with them. If you do not have enough information about others, it might affect your relationships with them. So gossiping sometimes is good for you. It can also make you feel happy more than I can express here. My gang knows it right. If you arte reading this book you are already in my gang. No Excuses.(Winking emoji dropped).

So, why be sad go and gossip about that lady or the person that makes you feel sad, don't worry you can feel guilty later.

CHAPTER FORTY

CLEANING

Nobody loves cleaning the mess when someone asks us to do but whenever we are alone at home, the Shanta Bai in us is automatically activated and we start cleaning everything by ourselves and when the cleaning is done we go outside the room, open the door as if we didn't do it and see everything so clean and clear that the only trash left is us. Never mind, I don't relate it to anyone but me. I always feel so. (crying emoji here.) Cleaning is the fastest way to keep ourselves happy, dirty environment makes us feel sick and sad too.

There is no denying that a clean environment feels better. Whether you are trying to clean up your own home to feel happier or clean up your face to feel happier and more confident, the choice is all yours. A happy home is a clean home, don't you think?

I'm not telling you to do it for your roommate, boyfriend, or girlfriend. I'm telling you to do it for yourself. You deserve to live in a clean place and feel happy.

Don't wait, get up clean your space, and reward your health with a clean and clear environment. You deserve it champ.

I will not repeat the lines here, do it yourself.

CHAPTER FORTY-ONE

RE-DECORATE YOUR ROOM

How long has it been since you changed your room's interior? How long has it been since you posted those stickers on the wall? Ever thought about changing your room's interior. I know Money is the issue, but see here we don't need to cash just some good ideas and a fresh happy mind. You can move your bed from one side to another and the study table can keep from one side of the room and the mirror you have kept in front of your bed can be moved to the brightest side of the room for the best mirror selfies.

This way your room is going to look different, you will have different feelings when you enter after changing the stuff here and there. And the happiness will be uncountable.

Renovating our room is a good thing to do when we feel overwhelmed by everything on our plate. Our room can be a heaven for us, a place where we can go to escape the stress of the world outside. It is where the heart is.

So why not give it a new life?

The way you decorate your room affects your happiness level. Your room should be a peaceful and happy place to retreat after a hard day of classes. Is your room making you depressed? Do you think we can renovate our room to change that? If so, let's go!

Well, can I repeat my words...

Get up champ, get up. Why are still being sad, just get up and renovate your room to feel happy inside.

CHAPTER FORTY-TWO

COUNT ON THE LITTLE THINGS

The cutest chapter.

Why should we count on little things to feel happy? As kids we are always so busy fighting for our rights, to go out, to get bigger toys and sports. But the happiness we used to have when playing with the little things of the early years was greater than anything the toys could do to us. Having a doll and playing with it, reading a book, and imagining these scenarios with friends is like writing the script of a movie. We are the actors and actresses, we are in control and feel relaxed because it is someone else.

Ever wonder why we count on such little things to feel happy! It is because we have come to expect less from life. Ever notice how you feel happier on a windy day? We all know the reason why. It's because we count on little things to be happy in our lives.

Little things make us happy, and we count on them to make a positive difference in our lives. The more of these little things we have, the happier we are.

Do you ever stop to think about the little things in life that make you feel happy? Like a good haircut, or a perfectly clean bathroom. Well, there are lots of small things that make us feel happy, but we tend to take them for granted when they're always there. So next time you get completely devoured by depression, think about how nice it is to have clean nails!

I will conclude this chapter here because I want you all to think and enjoy all the little things you have in your life.

CHAPTER FORTY-THREE

BE GREATFUL

Why should we be always grateful to feel happy? Being grateful is a big achievement, I promise. I know my promise does not matter but if I have written this, it makes sense to me, I have experienced this. Never stop being grateful to feel happy. Find out why it's important the next time you're in a bad mood and have the moment spoiled by a friend who thinks complaining is some sort of healthy, mature way of managing problems. You know, Happiness is a no-brainer. It's good for you and others. You feel good and so does everyone else, just be happy!

We have to be grateful to feel happy. Not everyone has it. We should thank god to be happy. If we laugh, we must laugh happily not laugh at others' expense. It doesn't mean that you are laughing at somebody, but you want to fool him/her by making him/her happy, or if your happiness makes him/her happy. So, remember to thank god for being able to be happy.

Somehow, If you are confused on how to be grateful, I will drop an example here;

I feel very grateful that I can sit on a chair. I can jump, sit and sleep on it. I feel very grateful that it could help me to support many other living things. I feel very grateful that my parents gave me the gift of the chair when I was born, which is a necessary item in human life!

Next time you feel sad just remind yourself how you are blessed with all the things around you and be more grateful for everything you have.

CHAPTER FORTY-FOUR

DONATE

You have a closet full of clothes that you never wear. You have family heirlooms that have been sitting in the attic for years. You have so many unused toys and those colors which you hardly use now. Why don't you donate your things to feel happy?

Why should we donate our things to feel happy? Because it is a great way to feel better and spread joy without spending money. You can get into the habit of donating just a few items and start feeling happier.

When people donate their unwanted possessions for charity, it makes them both happier and less materialistic. Sounds pretty good, right?

Did you know that when we do good deeds we feel happy inside? And when we help others we stay young longer and our lives are more meaningful. So why is it that so many people hold on to stuff that their family or friends could use but don't ask for? Maybe because they are very shy at asking but you can be the great one, you can donate it to them or call it a gift. You can donate it to the needy people whatever thing you have and you don't use can be used to some needy, am I right?

And If you think that cleaning your house makes you feel happy, I've got a question for you. What's better than donating your things to make you happier? Huh?

Well, why be sad when you can donate your old stuff to make someone else and yourself happy?

CHAPTER FORTY-FIVE

COMPLETE A TASK

Be honest with me, how many assignments are pending? And how much homework are you done with? Does it make you feel happy?

Obviously no, right? Why don't you take a long breath and start completing your tasks? It isn't that bad, I promise.

Sounds like a plan, hah! But do you want to feel good about yourself? Because if you don't complete your tasks and feel good about them, someone else will. Cheaply made and affordable, This chapter is the answer to most of your problems.

You want to be happy, I want you to be happy, everyone wants to be happy. But what can you do? Just complete the tasks and find joy, find happiness, find your mind at peace. And start seeing progress.

To feel happy, we must first accept the fact that most of who we are and what we do depends on the choices we make in life and the standards we set for ourselves. No one else can define for us what is good or bad, right or wrong, important or insignificant – at least not for long. Whether it's at home, at school, at work, or in sport – things only get better if you're willing to put in some effort."

I know you can do it. I promise you just make a little bit of effort and you will be counted under the happiest people around the globe.

CHAPTER FORTY-SIX

READ OLD CHATS

It is an real life experience. I have always felt happy whenever I tried reading old chats with my close people.

But I'll never know the reason why we read the old chats to feel happy. But I have seen many people doing this. Maybe when you have nothing to do, then you open your chat history and start reading your old chat with your friend(s). It's just like reading a novel. Before starting reading the chats, maybe you will realize how funny they are. Different things happen to different people every day, so some people want these funny things to get back into their memory, so it can make them feel happy and relieved.

We all know that chatting with your friends on Facebook can make you feel happy and even more connected with them. Imagine when you thought that your best friends had been kidnapped by aliens and you then read out all the old chats among you, their family, and friends for their safe return. It will be extremely funny to hear the funny stories, isn't it? Isn't it too much, yes yes it is? I should stop here.

Take your phone and start reading the old chats, you will not regret or maybe you will if you start reading those heartbreak chats. It's up to you, I am here to assist you only.

CHAPTER FORTY-SEVEN

A SMALL PICNIC

I like picnics. I like picnics because when you are on a picnic with someone you love, it can be fun. Like two people on a date or something. You could be thinking about how much you love them and things like that. Plus, if you go by yourself, you get to eat all the cake!

Small picnics are not just for small people! Go on, invite yourself to a small picnic, you'll be happy you did. You are judging me right now, aren't you? I mean we can spend a little on ourselves for our happiness, right? You don't have to spend big cash on a small picnic, that is why it is called a small picnic. Is it all making sense now?

When you have some great plans for doing nothing. So you should organize an indoor picnic get-together, As you all know that going for a picnic means that you need to go outdoors and at that too you will be lost after some time.

Whereas if you are sitting indoors, you will not even require GPS or maps because you know the exact location of everything and thus you can easily move everywhere at your own expense. Are you satisfied now, huh? You can do it alone too, just a tip. (The emoji with glasses dropped).

Yes, whenever you feel sad just buy yourself some chips make a friendly ambiance, and make yourself feel the happiest.

CHAPTER FORTY-EIGHT

LAUGHING EXERCISE

Have you seen those ages uncle aunties outside your home laughing like someone is tickling them? Have you seen how happy they look while doing this? That's how we buy happiness without cash!!

Sometimes I love to be silly and laugh at my jokes. When I'm with my friends, they like to do this too. We enjoy being silly and laughing together because it feels funny and happy. Laughing is fun and healthy. So when you're with your friends and family, why not practice laughing together? What a piece of nice advice, right? To add some entertainment and happiness to our life, we can try laughing regularly. It's effective enough. Laughing exercise is one of the most effective ways to help you smile and relieve stress. Also, it could strengthen your heart which is good for your health.

Also, Laughing is the best way to relax oneself. It enables one to forget daily stress and pressures. Laughing is just like medicine. People who are always laughing are usually healthier. Laughter also boosts the immune system, strengthens our bones and muscles, improves our circulation, and cleanses our bodies of stress-related toxins. So next time you're feeling tired and worn out, do the following activity for 10 minutes, which will help keep your heart healthy and fit.

It's cost-free, completely cost-free.

What are you waiting for then?

BUY NEW THINGS

This is my favorite chapter too guys. Well, anything that costs money is my favorite thing to be happy about? Did I just break my promise on how to buy happiness without using cash? I guess I did but it's everyone's favorite right? Who doesn't like buying new stuff? That's the other question that we are broke, but who does not like having a room full of new things? Are you getting this feeling? That new dress, the new shoes, that pair of gloves and socks.

It's no secret that we're always looking for something new. You'd think it would be a solid indication of our happiness, but in fact, we tend to get excited about that new thing before we even get it.

The happiness when we scroll down things online and keep craving about them and sometimes those things even keep coming in our dreams. And then the happiness when we finally get that thing. I mean, I have no words to express that feeling.

Rest you know everything about this topic because I know we are all together in this. (Cat laughing emoji here).

The book is finally coming to an end so first complete it and then go buy yourself a new t-shirt, or a bottle straw or anything you like.

ALWAYS SAY THANK-YOU

Do not think much about it, just say thanks even for the little things too. It makes you happy and the other person too. People who say "thanks" for something will be happier than those who don't. This is because we have just made an emotion with gratitude. Say thanks whenever you are happy. It is probably not research but it is true, I guarantee, because if you have come this far reading, you might have started trusting me too?

What if people start saying that weird things make them happy? Like, "I'll just say thank you and smile since it makes me happy!" Or my favorite, when talking about something that didn't go well, "This case is a proven example of how saying thank you makes me feel happier than getting my way."

Cheer up, say thanks every time you feel like saying it. Don't worry the other person will be happier than you.

CHAPTER FIFTY-ONE

YOU

Okay, so this is the last and the shortest chapter of this Book.

I want to end all this by saying, LOVE YOURSELF, no matter how hard the time is, just LOVE YOURSELF. And don't let anyone harm you by their words or actions.

You are strong, and you are worth everything you want.

You deserve everything you ever wished for.

You deserve to be HAPPY all the time.

Don't let anyone fool you by saying happiness is temporary.

Happiness is permanent when you believe.

People you should be proud of: YOU

People you should love the Most: YOU

The most beautiful person in this world: YOU

Oh, look at YOU.

YOURSELF.

LIFE IS GOOD.

I LOVE YOU, JUST BE HAPPY.